WEDGE

Define Your Niche, Grow Your Business

"A 4-Step Process for Establishing Your Business' Place in a Competitive Market"

Julie Chavanu

Wedge: Define Your Niche, Grow Your Business

By Julie Chavanu, Founder, The Idea Compass

© Julie Chavanu, 2024

All Rights Reserved.
No Part of this publication may be reproduced, distributed or transmitted in any form or by any means including photocopying, recording or other electronic or mechanical methods without the express written permission of the author of this book.

Other than for personal and non-commercial use in your own home or in the case of brief quotation of a page example that is included in a review as permitted by copyright law.

Your First Steps

GET STARTED!

So, what's FIRST?

This is a **workbook**! It's meant to be written in, so pull out your *pencils* and get started!

Find more tools & keep learning by reading my newsletter at theideacompass.com. OR…

…to go to The Idea Compass newsletter.

Why define *Your Wedge*?

Defining your wedge is how you start creating your map of the direction you want your business to head.

Here, you'll create a Starting Point Sentence describing your initial business idea, you'll study a few Inspo-Competitors, you'll consider what's missing and how your idea is (even slightly) different than what's in the market now, and then you'll create an updated description of your customer and product or Your Wedge.

But that's just the tip of the iceberg! This workbook can be used over and over to help you keep a pulse on your industry and to help you stay one step ahead – in an easy and organized way – about shifts you may need to make in your business. This is working 'on' your business, not just 'in' it.

Using this workbook will help you do it on the regular.

This is your framework for looking at the marketplace – quickly and in a consistent way – so that you can track trends your niche over time.

Why do you even need to define *Your Wedge*?

- To move forward with confidence and stop second (and third) guessing yourself.
- To create clarity about how you can apply your expertise and experience in your niche.
- To create products that better address your customers' needs.
- To save your business time & money in both product development and marketing.
- To give yourself a tool to better understand why something isn't working, or…why it is.
- To more easily shift and pivot when your business needs to.
- The list goes on…but in a nutshell…this knowledge will empower you!

The Idea Compass

STEP 1:

Your Starting Point Sentence

The beginning is the most important part of the work.

-Plato

STEP 1:

Your Starting Point Sentence

You'll start these 4 steps with a Starting Point Sentence (SPS). This is your first, basic description of your business. It doesn't need to be too detailed, just a basic description, something like:

- I help new dog owners train their dog to 'go' outside.
- I help businesses manage their email marketing.
- I offer travel itineraries in the U.S.

You may have more detail, and that's okay too, it's just not necessary at this point to have all the details ironed out. That's what this research is for, to help you define your unique wedge within your niche using some basic internet searches and combining that with your own experience and expertise.

When you use a mapping app, it will ask you for your starting point and your end point. Think of this Starting Point Sentence as the starting point the GPS is asking you for. It's necessary for planning your trip and your business' next steps!

Write the 1st version of your **Starting Point Sentence** here:

STEP 1:

Your Starting Point Sentence

Next, copy your **Starting Point Sentence** into Google search, but *before hitting Enter*, **note down the list of words and phrases Google suggested for autofill words and phrases.**

These are keywords that you may not have considered or known about, but they are keywords that others (including potential customers) are actually searching for!

These are the trends in your niche, so take note of them now and any time you do a search on your niche or your business topics. They'll give you valuable information about search activity in your industry.

Note those words/phrases here:

STEP 2:

Your Inspo-Competitors

"Healthy competition fuels innovation, drives progress, and leads to breakthroughs."

— Sundar Pichai, Interview with WIRED (2017)

STEP 2:

Your Inspo-Competitors

What are Inspo-Competitors? They are businesses that may have inspired you to start your own business. They may be operating in the larger niche that you are looking to operate in.

It's likely they are also – in some ways – your competition. This isn't a bad thing. Competition simply means that people are making money in your niche. **This is great news!**

Here in **Step 2**, we are going to take a close look at those businesses already in the market. As a business owner or as someone just starting out, this is honestly a tough step. Most of us would prefer to just skip right over this step! It's hard to take a close look at what the competition is doing…and doing well. If anything, it's intimidating! **But…stay with me here.**

On the following pages, note down:

- The names of the inspo-competitors
- Their website
- Taglines
- And a quick, one-sentence summary of who these inspo-competitors' target audiences appears to be.

Also note what they sell:

- Courses, books or physical products
- Affiliate products (complementary products from other businesses)
- Advertising or sponsorships
- Note also the prices they charge (if available).

STEP 2:

Your Inspo-Competitors

This list will include inspo-competitors you are already aware of and some that you learned about in your search in Step 1.

What do they have? How do they operate?

Include things your competitors have that you currently don't…a big audience, a seemingly large marketing budget, a well-established blog or brand, a cool sponsor or influencer partner. Whatever it is that they have, include it in your notes.

The right wedge

Why?

Knowing these things will help you define the **RIGHT wedge for you and the RIGHT place to start** building your business. When you know and understand what's out there, and how these other businesses are operating, the slightly different path that will help you build in *your wedge* in the market will become clear. This information will help you **define** your own wedge.

You're looking for the **RIGHT wedge** for **YOUR business**. And, keep in mind, you only need one wedge to get started…

STEP 2:

Your Inspo-Competitors

Who are your Inspo-Competitors, what do they do, how do they do it?

Look for: Websites, taglines, a quick, one-sentence summary of who these inspo-competitors' target audiences are.

What do they sell? Courses, affiliate products, ads on their website. What prices do they charge (if available)? Write them here and/or add them to the spreadsheet.

Inspo-Competitor 1

Inspo-Competitor 2

The Idea Compass

STEP 2:

Your Inspo-Competitors

More Insp-Competitors:

> Inspo-Competitor 3

> Inspo-Competitor 4

The Idea Compass

STEP 3:

Consider Your Difference

"Be yourself; everyone else is already taken."

-Oscar Wilde

STEP 3:

Consider Your Difference

This step will take a bit more time and it really is where the rubber meets the road! This is your *thinking* step and the best thing you can do for yourself and your business is to be as objective as possible here. It isn't easy, but it *is* important!

As you start to think, you may decide that another **Inspo-Competitor needs to be added** to your list…or that one needs to be taken off. Adjust and update, but most importantly be thoughtful about your updates.

Make those notes and your reasons 'why' here in the worksheets for Step 3 (next pages).

As you make these notes and based on what you've learned so far, write down what *you* see as holes in the market. As you compared your Starting Point Sentence to the phrases and words Google tried to auto-fill, as you looked closely at the Inspo-Competitors on your list and what they are doing, **did you think everything was covered? Was something missing? Or, is there a space for something different?**

This is where you start (or continue) to form your perspective on the industry's white spaces, those wedges of service areas or products that aren't being fully addressed. **It's likely that the empty spaces you notice most are the ones that you know something about.** These are areas where you have experience (and can offer a solution) or have perspective on why a new/different solution will make a difference in the market.

It's also likely that your ideas/perspective will overlap some with your Inspo-Competitors. That's okay. Again, this isn't necessarily a bad thing.

You don't need a big wedge…just a little one…and you'll be on your way. You'll be on your way with a clearer head and a clearer plan.

So, let's keep moving…

The Idea Compass

STEP 3 (continued):

Editing & Distilling

Let's take a moment here to review your Starting Point Sentence. At this mid-way stage, are there edits you'd make yet?

The answer may be 'no'. We're not done yet and it's okay to say 'no' at this check-in point, so decide and just keep moving forward.

Want to edit your **Starting Point Sentence** yet? Remember, this is a one-sentence description of your business. Based on what you've learned, does it make sense to niche it further? Or maybe niche it less?

Being objective and realistic here will take you further, quicker!

> Do I need to edit my **Starting Point Sentence at this mid-way point**? Write or Re-write it here:

STEP 3 (continued):

Editing & Distilling

Do you need to add/remove any **Inspo-Competitors**?

Are there businesses you found that more closely match what you plan to do? Is there one on your current list that, based on what you found in your research, no longer needs to be on the short-list of competitors?

Again: Being objective and realistic here will take you further, quicker!

Are there any **Inspo-Competitors** I can add/remove? And why?

Are there any **Inspo-Competitors** I can add/remove? And why?

STEP 3 (continued):

Getting Clearer

With your Starting Point Sentence and an updated list of Inspo-Competitors, it's likely becoming **clearer to you** where your business fits into the current market picture.

You have clearer ideas about what's going on in your chosen niche/market and you have found or learned about a broader range of competitors.

All of that work and consideration has also probably made your head spin a little (or a lot)!

In this step, you'll stop that spinning and start **writing down more detail about what you see as missing in the market**. It may be little things; it may be big things. Capture them all.

Don't underestimate things that seem like small tweaks to what's in the market currently. These are the things that make a difference!

Remember to **pay attention to what you learned in Step 2**. Are there behaviors, phrases/terms, or **new trends** in your market niche that haven't yet been fully tapped into? Are there Inspo-Competitors **making shifts (small or large)** in what they are offering or talking about? What **problems** are people talking about that still need to be solved?

Let's go...

Pro Tip: To dive a bit deeper on what's missing in the market, find reviews of products/services in your niche and see what buyers are saying about it.

For instance, you can find reviews from both happy and unhappy customers. In those reviews, you can find more detail on what's missing in the market.

STEP 3 (continued):

Spaces in the Niche

What do **you see as missing in the market**?

Reminder: These differences do *not* need to be huge. Don't underestimate things that seem like small tweaks to what's in the market currently. These are the things that make a difference!

Remember to **pay attention to what you learned in Step 2 and here in Step 3**. Are there **behaviors, phrases/terms, or new trends** in your niche that haven't yet been fully tapped into? Are there Inspo-Competitors **making (small or large) shifts** in what they are offering or talking about? What **problems** are people talking about that still need to be solved? **What do you notice?**

The hard part about this step is actually writing something down. It can be hard to make a decision, saying yes to something – and no to something else. I get that!

What I do know is that – for better or worse – things are constantly changing. Now, you've got a tool to help you get your head around some of the changes in the market, you've got a tool to help you organize your observations and make sense of them so you can make the most of your business!

STEP 3 (continued):

Spaces in the Niche

Based on what you've learned in Steps 1 and 2 write your observations, ideas, and reflections here in Step 3. What angle or idea or perspective, as you see it, is missing?

STEP 3 (continued):
Spaces in the Niche, page 2

More space for thinking and reflecting…

STEP 4:

Define Your Wedge

"Opportunities don't happen, you create them."

-Chris Grosser,
founder of Upwork

STEP 4:

Your Wedge Statement

That was a LOT!

And really, this is a process you can use not only to start a business, but also to:

- **Expand into new products/services**
- **Re-visit as you plan your next quarter or next year**
- **Check-in when you feel shifts in your business and your niche**

Looking outside your own business on a regular basis is a very useful exercise. It keeps you well-informed – and a bit ahead of the game – as you navigate entrepreneurship. And now you've got a tool that makes the process easier.

Now, let's create your **Wedge Statement**.

This statement is your more refined Starting Point Sentence, one with more detail and one that you are creating with more confidence, information, and direction.

It's not set in stone, but this is where you are going to start. And you're creating it with open eyes and an informed perspective.

Key Points to remember:

- Include more detail than in your Starting Point Sentence in Step 1. You've got more detail and wider perspective, so use what you've learned.

- As part of that detail, niche down. Don't be afraid to narrow what you offer and who you offer it to; it's key to getting really good at what you do and what you are known for. As you grow, you can 'niche back up' if you need or want to, but with any limit on resources (time/money), you'll make much more progress by staying focused on 1 thing.

- In that same spirit, say no to some things. Note them down somewhere if you feel you'll forget something important but say no for now.

STEP 4:

Your Wedge Statement

Using what you've learned and your updated perspective on not just the niche, but also your unique experiences and perspectives, create Your Wedge Statement below:

This is what my business does (or will soon do), addressing a wedge in the niche that my business operates in:

My business offers this product(s)/service(s):

To this set of customers:

Taking advantage of my experience and expertise in:

Your Next Steps

CONGRATULATIONS!

So, what's next?

Understanding your wedge will help **create clarity** in how you develop new offers, speak to your customers, and plan in your business.

This exercise is **great to do regularly**. Including it as part of your business planning for the upcoming year is perfect. However, any time you consider additions or changes, this process will support your decision-making.

Keep learning by reading my newsletter at theideacompass.com. OR…

Scan me

…for The Idea Compass newsletter.

www.ingramcontent.com/pod-product-compliance
Lightning Source LLC
Chambersburg PA
CBHW062316220526
45479CB00004B/1196